D1489264

First published 1980
Macdonald Educational
Holywell House
Worship Street
London EC2A 2EN

© Macdonald Educational
1980

Adapted and published
in the United States
by Silver Burdett Company,
Morristown, N.J.
1981 Printing

ISBN 0-382-06446-1

Library of Congress
Catalog Card No. 80-53847

COVER The emperor is carried in
a palanquin from the city gate.

Editor
Diana Railton

Design
Robert Wheeler

Production
Rosemary Bishop

Picture Research
Jan Croot

Illustrators
Jeffrey Anderson/
  B. L. Kearley
Marion Appleton
John Bilham
Chan Yee Mee
Donald Harley/
  B. L. Kearley
Hayward Art Group
Douglas Kirk
Tony Payne
Amrik Sidhu
George Thompson

Consultants
Harry Strongman
Bulmershe College of
Higher Education,
England

Carolyn Blackman
Melbourne Church of
England Grammar School,
Australia

Photographs
Atkins Museum, William Rockhill Nelson Gallery of
    Art, Kansas City Mo.: 33(TL)
Bibliothèque Nationale, Paris: 31
Boston Museum of Fine Arts: 35
Trustees of the British Museum: 26, 34, 44
Camera Press: 47(B)
C.M. Dixon/Photoresources: 33(TR), 48(B)
Freer Gallery of Art, Washington DC: 33(B)
Werner Forman Archive: 27(T), 43, 48(T)
Giraudon: 22/23(T)
Robert Harding Associates: 32, 49
William Macquitty: 50
Tim Megarry: 8/9
National Palace Museum, Taipei: 23(B), 30, 47(T)
The Palace Museum, Peking: 27(B), 29
Snark International: 25

The publishers are grateful to the School of
Oriental and African Studies (University of London)
for their help with some of the photographs.

The publishers have been unable to trace the
copyright holder of the photograph on page 22(B)
and apologize for any breach of copyright.

The agricultural calendar on page 10 was adapted
from *China's Civilization* by Arthur Cotterell and
David Morgan (George G. Harrap and Co. Ltd,
London) with the kind permission of George G.
Harrap and Co. Ltd and Praeger Publishers, New
York.

The ancient Chinese

Lai Po Kan

The ancient Chinese

China is unique among the early civilizations in the world. This is because the culture developed by the ancient Chinese has been passed down from generation to generation to this very day.

The earliest Chinese settled in the Yellow River valley where the soil favoured the growth of their crops. However, the climate of the area was not always favourable. As time went by, the Chinese came to believe that they had to live in harmony with Nature in order to survive. Traditional beliefs like these are still very important to Chinese people today – almost 3,500 years later.

The small settlements in the Yellow River valley gradually grew into larger, organized states. By 1500 BC, China had become a kingdom. When the throne passed from father to son of one family, that family became known as a 'dynasty'. On pages 54–55 you can see the different dynasties that ruled China until AD 907. Often the term 'dynasty' refers to the period of time in which a family ruled. For example, the Shang dynasty embraces the period 1500–1027 BC.

From the Yellow River valley, the ancient Chinese spread southwards over an enormous area of land. It was difficult for one government to control so much territory. However, during the Han dynasty (206 BC–AD 220) and the T'ang dynasty (AD 618–907), China became more united than ever before. These dynasties were highlighted by inventions, such as paper making and printing, and enriched by poetry and art. They are often regarded as the greatest dynasties of all.

In this book, we shall step back into history and look mainly at the way of life of the Chinese people who lived during the Han and T'ang dynasties.

Contents

The first Chinese

The first Chinese lived in the North China Plain, along the fertile Yellow River valley, over half a million years ago. The Yellow River looks yellow because of a thick yellow soil, called 'loess', which it collects in the Gobi Desert and brings down to the valley. Over the centuries, the river has frequently flooded its banks leaving behind a lot of loess in the valley. Winds blowing from the Gobi Desert have dropped even more loess onto this area. The early people found that crops grew easily on the loess soil and so they settled on the plain.

Loess is very fertile when it is wet but, without rain or river flooding, it soon turns to dust. The climate of North China varied from year to year. Sometimes too much rain led to flooding. At other times too little rain caused droughts. There were also earthquakes. The early Chinese therefore found that their crops, and their lives, depended on the temper of the seasons, the amount of rainfall, and the level of the river. They grew to believe that they must live in harmony with Nature in order to prevent harmful happenings.

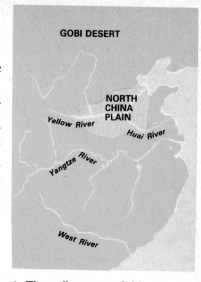

▲ The yellow part of this map shows the area around the Yellow River valley where the first Chinese lived.

▼ The early Chinese grew grain on terraces which are still used by farmers today.

By 4000 BC, there were many large settlements along the Yellow River valley. The people farmed and hunted, and stored food for the winter. They also made cooking pots and storage jars from clay. They often decorated these with various symbols that could have developed later into Chinese writing. It was necessary for them to guard their possessions from raiders. A ditch for defence was therefore built around the settlement and the inhabitants would take up arms against an enemy's attack. Settlements gradually grew into small states led by chiefs. The most powerful chief became king and ruled over a large part of the North China Plain. The kingship was often passed down a family from father to son.

As the population increased, the early Chinese began to move southwards into the valleys of the Yangtze River and the West River where the climate was less harsh. The many different peoples who were already living in those areas became influenced by the Chinese way of life. By the year 221 BC, China had become united as an empire under the Ch'in dynasty (see page 54). After the Ch'in dynasty the Han dynasty lasted from 206 BC–AD 220. Four centuries later, the T'ang dynasty reunited China and ruled from AD 618–907.

▲ In about 4000 BC the Chinese made pottery and decorated it with special designs (1). Inside the cooking pot (2), three different dishes could be prepared at once. The pot on top was used for cooking food with steam.

Farming

The Chinese empire covered an enormous area. The farmers' lives therefore varied according to the local climate and soil. Because they were so afraid of drought, they built a system of canals so that river water could spread over large areas of land. The most important crops grown in the north were wheat and millet. In the south, because there was more rain and sun, rice was grown in 'paddy fields' that were flooded with water. Most of the farmers' work was in the fields but many grew mulberry trees so that the women could keep silkworms and make clothes. Farmers who lived near the towns or villages might grow various types of vegetables, seasonings (like ginger) and fruit to sell in the markets.

▼ A Chinese farming calendar which was used in northern China in about AD 100. It was drawn up, by a government official, in accordance with the movement of the moon, stars and earth. Each month began with the new moon. The Chinese farmers would follow the instructions on the calendar for all the jobs that they and their families had to do. It also told them when they should carry out certain religious ceremonies.

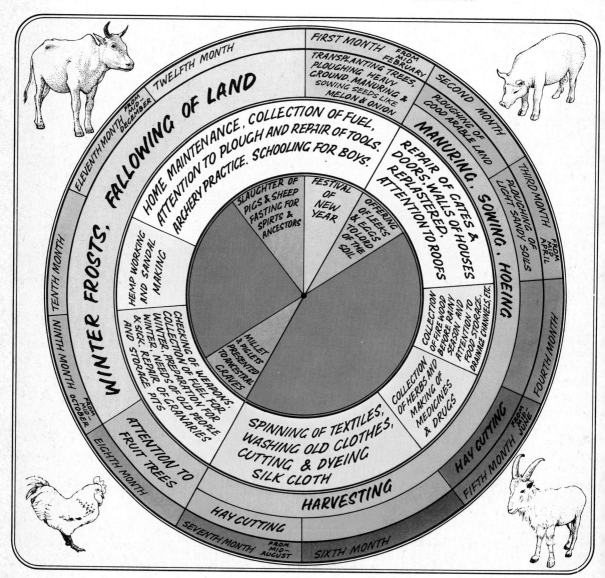

▲ Paintings like these were drawn during the Han dynasty. They showed several aspects of the farmers' work. The one above shows a plough being pulled by two oxen. Before seeds could be planted, all the land had to be ploughed. Even the terraced fields, like those on pages 8-9, were ploughed.

The farmers were expected to supply the nobles with game. They therefore had to find time to go hunting for animals like deer, and birds, with the aid of falcons, hounds, and bows and arrows.

Most farmers were lent a plot of land, either by the government or by a rich land owning family. In return, these farmers would have to give their landlord a large share of the produce they grew. Usually a government tax collector would come to claim this. Every farmer had to serve the government for a month each year by building or repairing roads, bridges or fortifications in various parts of the empire. In an emergency, he would have to join the army for as long as was necessary.

During the Han dynasty (206 BC–AD 220), farming improved because of the development of iron tools which were much more efficient than wooden or bronze ones. The population was growing rapidly and it was important that more food should be produced to meet the extra demand.

11

City life

Since the earliest times, cities in China have been teeming with people and bustling with activities. Because the ancient Chinese believed that the earth was square, most cities were built in the shape of a square. Every city was protected against attack by a strong wall which was built all the way round it, and the people could only go in and out through guarded gates. The streets were straight. They criss-crossed through the city from north to south and east to west, dividing the houses into enclosed areas called 'wards'.

The most famous of all ancient Chinese cities was Ch'ang-an. It was chosen by many emperors, including the Han and T'ang, as their capital. In the north of the city was the emperor's palace and audience hall. In the houses nearest to the emperor lived the nobles and officials. The ordinary people were crowded together in small houses in the wards. These had walls built round them. At night the gate of each ward was closed so that no one could get in or out. By the seventh century AD, over one million people lived in the city which covered about 77 square kilometres. As the population was so great, even the wealthy could not have very large houses. But each house still had a courtyard, however small.

▼ A plan of the city of Ch'ang-an, capital of the Han and T'ang emperors, constructed as a square-shaped grid. The three gates in each wall open onto straight main streets. Can you spot the two large market places in the centre?

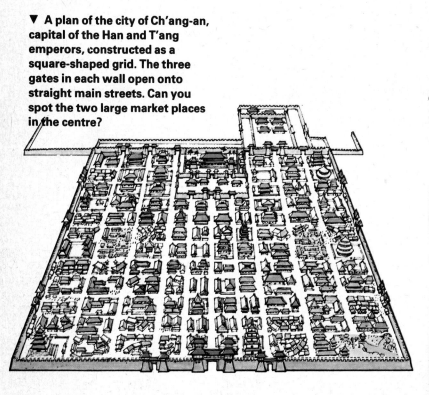

The most important part of a city was the market place. It was opened at noon each day with several drum beats. Farmers, craftsmen, bakers and traders would all display their goods. Barbers, scribes and fortune-tellers offered their services in the midst of the busy traffic and din.

Travellers and the men of the city would meet in the wine shop. They would buy a cup of wine for a small sum and pass the time talking with friends. Or they could watch dancers, singers, jugglers and acrobats perform outside. Often the local story teller would earn a little money by telling them tales.

The family

A Chinese household was normally very large. This was because the grandparents, parents and children of one family all lived together. It was considered a sign of good luck and happiness if as many as five generations were living together at one time. A Chinese man's home was his anchor. However far away he had to go, he would always return to his family in times of trouble.

The houses of the very rich were made from wood with a roof of tiles. They were more than one storey high and had a lot of elaborately decorated rooms. But the poor people's houses had only a few small rooms made from wooden planks or mud, covered with a roof of bamboo or reeds. Rich Chinese ladies lived in their own rooms at the back of the house and did not come into contact with male strangers. But there was not enough space in the poor people's houses for the women to have their own rooms.

Boys, as the family's heirs, were more highly regarded than girls. Boys and girls would play together until they became teenagers when they were separated. When a boy was about 20 years old, he was considered an adult and his hair was ceremoniously pinned up under a cap. But a girl was considered an adult at the age of 15 when a ceremony would also be held to pin up her hair.

▲ As the houses of the common people were so small, often most of the family would sit outside in the courtyard. In this scene, you can see some of the different activities that featured in Chinese family life. Women are busy preparing cloth, while two elderly men exchange opinions. A group of boys read from a scroll, and the younger members of the family play together. A servant carries home a sack of grain from the market.

Marriages were arranged by parents and friends. Young people were not allowed to meet and make their own choice. When a man married, his wife would leave her family to live with her husband's. It was the strict rule in the family that younger people must respect and obey older people. The wife's duty was to serve her parents-in-law and her husband, and to look after the children. Nearly every family, however poor, had servants who had been either hired or bought.

A man could marry again when his wife died, but a widow would not unless she was extremely poor. A girl whose fiancé died was often expected to look after her dead fiancé's parents and not to marry any other man.

15

Chinese food and drink

Chinese city-dwellers relied on the hard-working farmers in the countryside to provide them with food. The most important cereal foods were millet, wheat and rice. Cattle, goats, sheep, pigs, chickens and ducks, and even dogs, were kept for meat. Some farmers specialized in providing fish. The servants did most of the shopping in the market. Often they bought a whole animal and cut it up themselves at home. The rich nobles enjoyed going hunting in their spare time. They would catch many animals, such as bears and deer, which they would bring home and serve to their guests.

But for the poor, life was not at all easy. They would be lucky if they had enough to eat. The only times they ate meat were at festivals or weddings, and perhaps during a very old person's special birthday celebrations. When fresh meat was not available, eggs, salted or dried fish, and cabbage preserved in salted water, were sometimes served instead. Their normal diet consisted of a stew of vegetables. In the north, they would eat a bowl of millet with the stew; in the south, a bowl of rice.

▲ In a rich family's kitchen, the servants are busy preparing a meal. The meat and vegetables have been bought from the market. On the left you can see a charcoal stove.

CHOPSTICKS

Chopsticks have to be held firmly between the thumb and second and third fingers of the right hand. They can then meet at the bottom to pick up food.

The rich people in the cities often used to entertain their friends at enormous expensive banquets. The meal might begin with a stew of ox, pig, deer or dog or, sometimes, of camel's feet! One course after another would then be served on fine porcelain bowls and plates. Other dishes included snail, turtle, young goat and bear's paws. Various kinds of fish were either cooked whole, sliced or minced. Favourite vegetables were bamboo shoots and lotus roots. All these foods were eaten with chopsticks, made from bamboo, wood, horn or ivory. At the end of the meal, fruits like tangerines and lichis were served.

Alcohol was often made from millet and rice. Wine made from grapes was first introduced in the Han dynasty. The wine was poured from large jugs decorated with gold or silver, and drunk out of goblets with silver or golden handles, or lacquered cups. In the T'ang dynasty, vineyards were cultivated in areas where the soil and climate were suitable. At that time tea, which later became China's most important beverage, was introduced to many different households.

▼ From the kitchen, smartly dressed servants bring steaming dishes of food and wait on the members of the family during their meal. On the table on the right two whole fish, garnished with vegetables, are about to be served. The man is drinking wine from a lacquered cup. On the small table there is a wine jug from which the servants will refill the cups. From the paintings that have been found in old tombs, we know that men and women often used to have their meals together during the Han and T'ang dynasties. At the back of the room you can see two orange trees. These were probably given to the family by friends at Chinese New Year in order to wish them happiness and prosperity.

Traditional beliefs

The ancient Chinese believed that many spirits lived in mountains, streams and trees, in the air, wind, thunder and rain, and in other things. In order to make sure that the spirits were pleased with them, and would protect them from harm, the Chinese worshipped them and offered them food and drink. Special people, called 'shamans', claimed to be able to talk to the spirits. The ordinary people therefore used to ask the shamans to pass on their messages to the spirits.

The Chinese also worshipped gods who were responsible for different things. For example, the earth god provided good soil; another god looked after the millet. In the sky there was a supreme god who was both just and powerful. But the god who watched over the people all the year round was the kitchen god. He gave reports of their behaviour to the supreme god on New Year's Eve.

Another important Chinese tradition was ancestor worship. The people believed that the spirit of a dead man or woman could control the welfare of the rest of the family still living. The only way a family could please its ancestors was by praying to them and offering them food and drink. In every Chinese house there was a special hall where the spirits of the dead ancestors were thought to live. The family would worship them on the anniversaries of their death and birth, and during particular festivals.

▲ Apart from believing that they had to worship spirits and gods, the ancient Chinese thought that the universe depended on the balance of two forces — Yin and Yang. Yin stood for dark, weak, female, night, moon and Earth. Yang stood for bright, strong, male, day, sun and Heaven. The symbol above represents the idea that they must balance. If they did not, evils such as droughts or floods might occur. This belief dates back to the time when the first Chinese settled in the Yellow River valley and tried to live in harmony with nature.

►The Chinese tried to balance Yin and Yang by carefully choosing sites for buildings and burial grounds. If a bad site were chosen, the spirits would be offended and cause much evil. The picture shows a specialist choosing a site with a magnetic compass.

In the hall where the spirits of
the dead ancestors live, the
different members of the
family take turns to worship
them. The head of the family
leads the ceremony by
kneeling down three times and
tapping his head on the floor
nine times. Incense is being
burnt and offerings of food
have been placed on the altar.
On the two tablets in the
centre of the altar are written
the names and dates of birth of
the different ancestors.

Leisures and pleasures

The ordinary people worked very hard indeed on the land or in the towns. But they had little money to spend on entertainments. However, both they and the rich nobles enjoyed watching various performances that would often be held in the local market place. On these occasions they could listen to story tellers, musicians and singers, and watch jugglers, sword dancers, magicians, fire eaters, tightrope walkers and acrobats display their tricks. On festival days such performances would continue all day.

Rich and poor all enjoyed cock fighting, kite flying, and ball and shuttlecock games. In the city of Ch'ang-an, the favourite place for everyone to stroll, or have picnics, or just look at others, was in the public park beside the lake. You can see it in the diagram on page 12, in the south-east corner. Besides hunting outings, the nobles held noisy parties and banquets that often continued well into the night and sometimes until dawn.

▲ A festival is being celebrated in a village in China. In the market place, in front of the temple, a special platform has been constructed and a troupe of dancers and musicians are performing. Among the crowd, jugglers and acrobats display their tricks. These performers earn their living by travelling from one village to another on request from the villagers. In the houses in the village compound at the back, you can see the red lucky signs that were stuck up on Chinese New Year. Some of the children are flying paper kites that the Chinese invented in the second century AD.

Other enjoyable activities for all were the family gatherings that took place on festivals. New Year's Day was the most important festival. Every family would stick new signs, written on red paper, on both sides of the doors of their houses. Only happy and lucky sayings were allowed so that bad luck did not come to the family. Special food would be prepared and everyone would try to be at home to celebrate. Children, wearing their best clothes, would take gifts of sweets and fruits to their family's friends. By the T'ang period, gunpowder had been invented and firecrack· ers made from it. They were exploded in front of every house in order to drive away the evil spirits and make a clean start to the new year.

Another enjoyable festival for children was held in Mid-Autumn on the night when the moon was supposed to shine the brightest. All the children would light brightly coloured lanterns and then hang them up in their courtyards.

▼ This game, called Double Sixes, was often played for hours at a time by both rich and poor. No one today knows what the rules were.

21

Confucius and Lao-tzu

During the Chou dynasty (1027–221 BC), the nobles grew very independent of the king and quarrelled and fought over land, regardless of whom it belonged to by law. The common people suffered great hardships from this and did not know where to turn. The educated people tried to think of ways to improve the situation. The man whose ideas lasted the longest was called Confucius (551–479 BC). During much of his lifetime, he travelled from one noble's court to another telling them how people ought to behave. He said that everyone should be loyal (especially to the ruler), sincere and polite, and respect and obey their parents. Most nobles would not listen to Confucius. However, later on, some of his disciples obtained very important government posts and could therefore put his teachings into practice. From the Han dynasty onwards, Confucius became honoured as the greatest teacher who had ever lived. He was worshipped in temples that were built all over the empire.

▲ Confucius, with some of his disciples, is consulted on taxation by an important noble. All Chinese governments have honoured the descendants of Confucius with pensions and noble titles. His family is one of the oldest in the world — today the 77th generation is living in Taiwan.

◄ Confucian temples were built in every town in China. This rubbing shows part of a very large one in Nanking. In the main temple building there is an altar to Confucius with a tablet similar to the ones on page 19. Confucianism continued to be very important to the Chinese until recently.

► This famous painting shows Lao-tzu leaving China on a buffalo. We can tell that the painting has belonged to many different people, including emperors, from the seal mark that each has stamped on it.

Another man whose theories influenced many people was Lao-tzu. He was older than Confucius but lived at the same period. Lao-tzu did not believe that it was possible to have a perfectly kind and just government. He disapproved of people who showed off, particularly in their appearance and during ceremonies. He especially did not like the lifestyle of the ruler's court! He believed that people should go back to leading a simple and natural life, without any government interference, and in harmony with Nature. 'Never interfere and let things take their natural course,' he said. Many of his followers left their homes and jobs in order to be alone to think more about Nature. Nature's Way was called the 'Tao' so these followers became known as 'Taoists'.

Lao-tzu became so disappointed by the events that took place during the Chou dynasty that he left his job and travelled west out of China. As he was leaving, one of the officers who was guarding the 'Pass' from China begged him to leave behind his teaching in writing. It is said that he agreed and wrote a book of about 5,000 words. This book was called 'Tao Te Ching' which means 'Nature's Way and its Power'. With the help of similar books, Taoism has been passed down among the Chinese from generation to generation until this very day. But no one knows what happened to Lao-tzu after he left China, or in which country he died.

The emperor

The early emperors of China, like the kings before them, claimed to be Sons of Heaven and to have the authority to govern all the Earth. But, with this privilege, each one became responsible for the welfare of the people.

Some emperors are famous for their achievements. You can read about them, as well as the one empress who ruled from AD 683-705, on pages 50-53. But others were rather lazy, even though they were meant to attend to all problems of government and make decisions. The main business was carried out by different officials who had been selected through examinations. Among many tasks, the officials were responsible for collecting taxes, directing building projects, deciding on punishments for different crimes, and compiling the calendar. The ordinary people, like the farmers, also had to be prepared to serve the government whenever necessary. The emperor received reports from his officials and made arrangements for the control of rebellions.

The emperor was expected to lead various ceremonies, the most important being those in which he begged Heaven and Earth for a good harvest. On the longest night of the year, dressed in a blue robe, he fasted all night and then prayed before dawn at a special outside altar. On the first day of spring, he ploughed a furrow in the grounds of his palace. Finally, on the longest day of the year, dressed in a yellow robe, he offered sacrifices in thanksgiving for the harvest his people had received.

▶ The second emperor of the T'ang dynasty, T'ai-tsung, listening to a scholar tell him about some of the texts that Confucius had taught from. The men around him are his government officials whose ranks are shown by the colour and pattern of their robes and the ornaments attached to their hats. Besides the emperor, no one could wear a whole robe of yellow; only the palace roofs could have yellow tiles.

▼ A reconstruction showing the front of the emperor's palace in Ch'ang-an (see the north-east of the diagram on page 12). A massive gateway and hall, and triple corner-towers, guard the entrance to the palace so that the emperor is well hidden from the public eye. Behind the thick walls, in richly decorated rooms, he is attended by his officials, advisers, servants and wives who look after all his needs. His officials and advisers have their offices in the outer part of the palace from where there is no access to the private inner area.

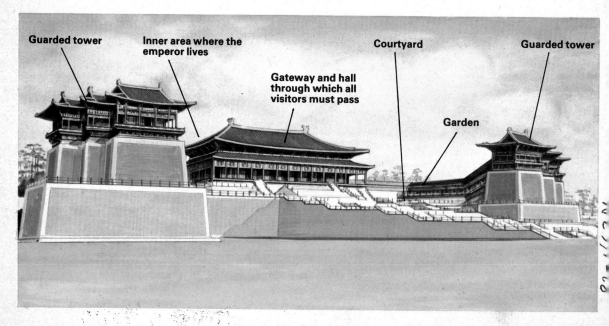

Guarded tower

Inner area where the emperor lives

Gateway and hall through which all visitors must pass

Courtyard

Guarded tower

Garden

Court life

In the private inner area of the emperor's palace at Ch'ang-an there were many enormous halls as well as apartments for the emperor himself, his family, and the hundreds of women that he liked to have around him. This area was enclosed by gardens and courtyards. Around the palace was a beautiful park which was full of rare birds and animals, ornamental towers and pavilions, and lakes. As well as the main palace in Ch'ang-an, the Han and T'ang emperors also had one in Loyang and summer and winter palaces in different parts of the country. In a grand procession the court would move with the emperor wherever he chose to reside.

The emperor was expected to start work very early each morning. However, because of the many distracting pleasures available at the court, some were less diligent than others. Each emperor's lifestyle depended on his own interests. All night parties were often held for the court. At these, a poet might be asked to write verses on the spot and then recite them one by one. Musicians, dancers, singers, acrobats and jugglers, would perform before the large audience. Sometimes many members of the court would go hunting on horseback with the emperor.

▲ This courtier is playing a clapper. His tunic and hat are typical of the T'ang period (AD 618-907).

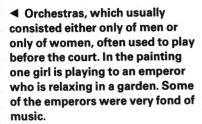

◄ Orchestras, which usually consisted either only of men or only of women, often used to play before the court. In the painting one girl is playing to an emperor who is relaxing in a garden. Some of the emperors were very fond of music.

► The emperor would rarely walk from one part of the palace to another. Instead he would be carried by many of his attendants, like Emperor T'ai-tsung in the painting here. As it was often very hot, the ladies around the emperor are waving fans to create a cool breeze. Important people could make appointments to speak before the emperor on his throne in the Audience Hall of the palace. Emperor T'ai-tsung welcomed all kinds of foreign influence into China. In turn, Chinese influence spread to countries such as Vietnam, Tibet, Korea and Japan.

Writing

Evidence of early Chinese writing has been found on animal bones and tortoise shells discovered in the Yellow River valley. They date back to about 1500 BC – the time of the Shang dynasty. The scholars who studied the signs say that they are questions addressed by the Shang kings to their ancestors, asking them if particular days were suitable for certain activities like hunting. They would scratch the signs onto the top surface of the bone or shell and then apply a hot metal stick to some holes drilled on the other side. The cracks that appeared were understood to mean either 'yes' or 'no'. Some of the marked bones and shells still survive today and are highly prized by museums in different parts of the world.

Many of these early signs were pictures that were easy to recognize. For example, the sun was represented by a circle with a stroke in it and the moon by a sort of crescent. You can see this in the diagram below. When the pictures of the sun and moon are put together, the whole symbol means brightness: 明 A tree is shown with a trunk, drawn as a vertical stroke, while the roots below are a curved stroke downwards and the branches above are a curved stroke upwards. When two trees are put together, the symbol means forest: 林 . Several thousand different pictures were used as words at that time. From them, modern Chinese writing gradually developed. Although many different languages are spoken in China, this one form of writing can be understood by all.

▲ An animal's shoulder bone, dating from about 1500 BC, on which words were written in the form of pictures. Can you recognize any? Chinese written words today, known as 'characters', developed from these early pictures.

▼ How some Chinese characters developed from early picture signs to less recognizable symbols that were put into a standard index after 213 BC.

	SUN	MOON	TREE	BIRD	HORSE
ABOUT 1500 BC	⊙	☽	米	🐦	🐎
BEFORE 213 BC	⊙	☾	朱	鳥	馬
AFTER AD 200	日	月	木	鳥	馬

28

► Chinese characters were written with a brush, held in the right hand, like the one this poet is holding. It would be dipped into ink which was made from a mixture of soot, from burnt pine trees, and glue

▲ Before the Chinese invented paper in AD 105, they used to brush their characters down wooden strips, like the ones above. When the whole column of one strip had been used, its surface would be cut off with a knife so that the clean surface below could be written on. When a piece of writing had been completed on a number of strips, they would be tied together with string and rolled into a book. The title was written on the front of the book.

During the Chou dynasty many new words were added to the script. But this caused confusion because there were many different ways of writing the same word. So, in 213 BC, the First Emperor of China ordered his chief official to issue an index listing 3,300 words which were to be used by everyone. During the Han dynasty, nearly 10,000 words were added to the standard index. Over the years, many more words have been added to the Chinese script. Today, most Chinese people are only able to read and write about three or four thousand words. A person with good handwriting is regarded very highly.

In the Chou and Ch'in dynasties, and the beginning of the Han dynasty, pieces of wood and bamboo were most commonly used for writing on. Silk was also used but, because it was expensive, it was reserved for only the most important documents. After paper was invented in China in about AD 105, books of paper could be made and these replaced the bulkier materials. Much effort was put into writing and copying books. They were regarded with great respect and carefully handed down the generations.

Education

The Chinese have always had great respect for learning. All parents tried to give their sons, rather than their daughters, as good an education as possible. In poor families, boys were usually trained from early childhood to do the same jobs as their fathers. However, very intelligent boys were sometimes able to go to school if a rich relative or group of neighbours agreed to pay the fees. Boys from wealthy families could either go to school or learn from a private tutor in their own homes. Girls of wealthy families might also learn at home from a private female tutor. Often a scholar would teach his own sons and daughters. Otherwise a girl would learn domestic tasks from her mother, like sewing and embroidery.

The main aim of schools was to train boys so that they could apply for entry to the government as an official. This meant passing a series of difficult examinations. In order to prepare for these, a boy would have to start his education at the age of eight. All pupils, until recently, had to learn by heart the most important texts which Confucius used in his teachings. They would then learn how to write Chinese characters with a brush. First they would have to trace red characters, provided in exercise books, in black. After many long hours of practice on each one, they would be able to produce exactly the same character on their own.

▲ A private tutor teaches the sons of a wealthy family in their own home. They are learning from text books in the form of paper scrolls. The older boy on the right has a scholar's knife tied to his belt for cutting away the surface of wooden strips (see page 29).

▼ The examination results were pinned up on the walls outside the Examination Hall in the capital. Many people, including relatives and friends, waited anxiously to see them. Some of the men who failed would try again. Others became teachers, doctors, or other specialists.

After about seven or eight years of study, the first public examinations could be taken in each boy's district. Those who passed could, after further study, take the second one at the largest town nearby. The third and final one was very difficult. The successful men were regarded as scholars and their names would be added to a waiting list for junior official jobs in various parts of the country. Once a scholar had obtained a job as an official, his promotion in the government depended on whether he was liked by his superior who could recommend him to the emperor.

▼ The third and final examination was supervised by the emperor himself in the capital. It was very important and only held every three years. The questions the emperor would ask included many on special subjects like government organization.

Art

From earliest times, the Chinese showed great skill and imagination in their art and painting. Evidence of this can be seen in the pottery made in about 4000 BC and decorated with different designs (see page 9 again).

From the Shang dynasty (1500-1027 BC), hundreds of bronze tools and vessels have survived. Museums all over the world proudly possess them. The vessels were used for containing the offerings made in important sacrifices and ceremonies to the spirit world. Each one had a very complicated shape with various designs engraved or moulded onto it. During the Chou and Han dynasties, bronze vessels and figures were still made but they were not as splendid as the Shang ones.

▼ This piece of bronze was found in a tomb which dates back to the Han dynasty. The artists would have needed great skill to mould the bronze into such a complex shape. The model shows the sort of horse and carriage that would have belonged to an officer. The canopy sheltered him from the sun and rain. On page 37 you can see one in use.

▲ A piece of jade that has been shaped into a disc, symbolizing Heaven. The ancient Chinese believed that, with its help, the emperor was able to communicate with Heaven.

▶ One of the glazed pieces of porcelain that would have been traded from China in the T'ang dynasty. Because of its fame, we now call porcelain 'china'.

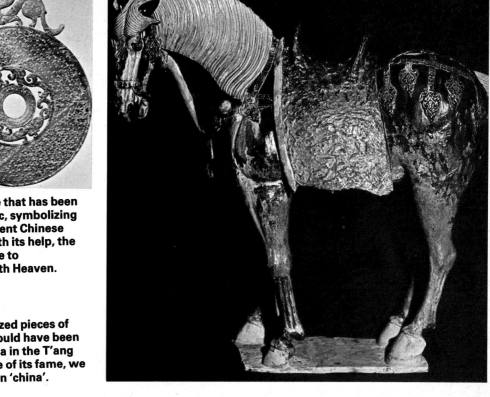

The very earliest pottery was shaped by the artists' hands. However, by 2000 BC, a wheel was being used by potters, enabling the objects to become more rounded. Very graceful, thin and delicate shapes were made. To cope with them, kilns that could hold high baking temperatures for several hours were developed. During the Shang dynasty, a fine white clay called 'kaolin' was discovered in many parts of China. When it is fired at very high temperatures, it becomes translucent and extremely hard. With the discovery of glazing, potters were able to perfect their skills. During the T'ang dynasty (AD 618–907), porcelain had become one of China's most valuable trading products.

Jade has always been prized in China as the most valuable of all precious stones. It symbolizes excellence and purity and has often been used in ceremonies. Elaborate processes were developed to carve it into different shapes, including animal figures and delicate vessels. During the Han and T'ang dynasties, jade was also worn by the rich as jewellery.

During the Han dynasty (206 BC–AD 220), lacquer was used more often for decorating wooden objects. It comes from the juice which is obtained from lac trees that grow in China. Many layers would be applied to objects, each one drying before the next was applied.

▲ A lacquered cup that would have been used by rich people (see page 17). Because lacquer is hard and long-lasting, it was often applied to articles in daily use, such as boxes and bowls, and to military equipment like shields.

The story of silk

The Chinese have certainly been making different coloured silks since 1500 BC. It is possible that they started to do so much earlier. From these ancient times, silk has been associated with industry and symbolizes virtue.

By the time of the Han dynasty (206 BC), the people living in the country had developed the best ways of rearing silkworms. All people with land to spare would grow mulberry trees around it and the women of their families would feed the leaves to the worms and then prepare the silk they produced. Much silk was supplied for the robes of the emperor and other wealthy people. (The poorer people could only afford to wear garments made from coarse cloth). But, before the invention of paper in the second century AD, silk was also used as a writing material for very special occasions, and important paintings were sometimes done on it. During the Han dynasty, silk became China's most popular trading product. Throughout the Roman world, she became known as the country of silk. The method of making silk in ancient China is shown below.

▲ Chinese designs on silk often consist of flowers and other symbolic objects. Different pieces of coloured thread are woven into one pattern.

◄ 1 First the leaves are picked from the mulberry trees that have been carefully cultivated by the men of the family.

▶ 2 Silkworms are reared by the women and kept together on special shelves where they are protected from the sun and rain. Every day they are fed as many mulberry leaves as they can eat.

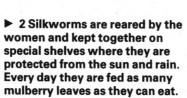

◄ 3 Each worm then produces a fine silk thread which forms a cocoon. The threads are soaked in hot water so that they can be lifted out individually with chopsticks and then wound on to reels. One thread might then stretch for several hundred metres. The small boy is blowing up the flames below the water cauldron.

34

▲ 4 Next the wound-up thread is twisted into strands on a spinning machine. This sort of machine was in use in China during the Han dynasty (206 BC-AD 220). China's machinery for cloth production was more advanced than that used in Europe, and other parts of the world, at the same time.

▲ 5 The different threads are dyed and then woven together on a hand loom, either into one plain piece or into coloured patterns. This was a very skilled job. However, the skill was acquired by many Chinese women when still young. Usually girls were taught how to spin at home by their mothers.

▼ 6 The newly woven silk is then pounded so that it becomes much softer. (The old painting showing this was done on silk.) Afterwards, the silk is ironed flat. The material would be sold and the required amount for clothing cut out from it. Compare the silk robes below with the poorer people's clothes on page 20.

A JEALOUSLY GUARDED SECRET

The Chinese people were instructed to conceal from foreigners their method of silk making, on punishment of death by torture. It was not until the third century AD that the secret leaked to Japan through Korea, and the Japanese were able to start making silk.

In the sixth century AD, two Persian monks smuggled some silkworm eggs and mulberry seeds out of China and took them to Constantinople. Gradually silk production spread over Europe where the delicate, expensive fabric was greatly treasured. However, silk making was not introduced to England until the 15th century.

Today China still produces some of the best quality silk in the world.

Defence

As the North China Plain around the Yellow River valley was so fertile, different people were always trying to seize parts of it. The possessions of its settlers would also be stolen. So, from the beginning, the early Chinese had to learn to protect themselves. By the time of the Chou dynasty (1027 BC), the states of China had built thick walls and watchtowers along the northern borders (see page 57). When the First Emperor of China had conquered all the other states, he realized that north Asian tribes were always looking for an opportunity to raid his empire. He therefore ordered that all the existing walls should be joined up into a single thick one. Thousands of men were ordered to work on this enormous task. Many died during the course of it. When the 'Great Wall' was completed, many years later, it was about 3,000 kilometres long and formed a solid barrier of defence between China and the north.

During the Han dynasty (206 BC–AD 220), all fit men between the ages of 23 and 56 had to serve in the army for two years. After that, they had to be prepared to join it whenever there was an emergency. When the T'ang dynasty came to power in AD 618, Emperor T'ai-tsung found that outside trouble lay more in the far west and north-east of China. It was necessary to send the army to protect China's borders there. As a result, fit men and boys were ordered to serve the army and go out to distant places. Some boys were not allowed to return home until they were grown men aged forty.

▼ The weapons China's soldiers used included daggers (1), swords (2), spears (3), lances with wooden shafts, knives, and bows and arrows. When iron began to be cast in about 700 BC, much stronger weapons could be made. Gunpowder was not used by the army until after the T'ang dynasty.

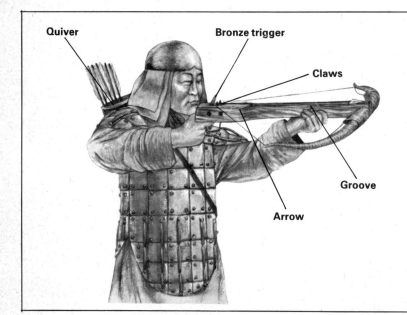

Quiver

Bronze trigger

Claws

Groove

Arrow

CROSSBOWS

In both the Han and T'ang dynasties, members of the army carried 'crossbows'. These weapons were very effective because each had a bronze trigger in the centre of the bow. When the soldier pressed the trigger, the claws holding the arrow in position would lower, sending it flying towards its target with much greater force than the ordinary hand bows. The picture also shows the type of armour a footsoldier would wear.

Members of the Chinese army on patrol around the Great Wall. They are wearing armour and helmets made from leather and bronze. The cavalry are carrying lances and shields. By the Han dynasty, stirrups were being used — a thousand years earlier than in Europe. An efficient 'breast strap' harness for horses had also been developed. The Great Wall had strong, square watchtowers at frequent intervals. Signals could be passed along from one tower to another. The top of the wall was wide enough for several horsemen to ride along together.

Trade

The early Chinese traded with one another by exchanging different products such as grain, vegetables, fruit, meat, cloth, silk, weapons and pottery. This is called 'bartering'. Bartering continued in China for a very long time until people found it more convenient to use money. At different times and places, objects such as stamped gold and bronze pieces began to be circulated as money. By the Ch'in dynasty (221 BC) bronze discs, with a square hole in the middle, were finally used by everyone all over the empire.

In 138 BC, the Han emperor sent a soldier called Chang Ch'ien to Central Asia. Chang Ch'ien brought back detailed information about goods that were available there, such as swift horses. China wanted some of these horses and the peoples of Central Asia and the Middle East wanted Chinese silk. And so trade began between them. The growing exchange of goods led to the opening of a route from Ch'ang-an across Asia to the Mediterranean. This route became known as the 'Silk Road'. In 106 BC, the first trading group from the west arrived in China.

▲ Some of the bronze coins used during the Han dynasty. The round ones were worth about 50 units. The one shaped like a knife was worth 500 units. The square hole in the centre of each allowed them to be strung together, often in hundreds.

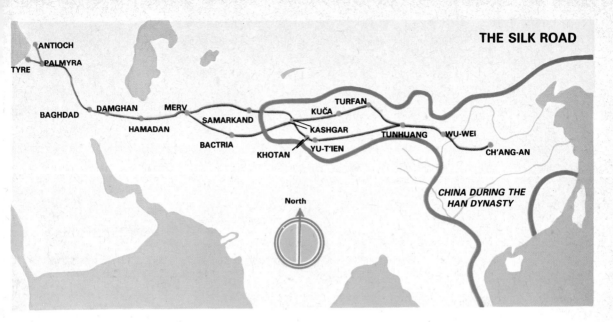

ANTIOCH
PALMYRA
TYRE
BAGHDAD
DAMGHAN
HAMADAN
MERV
SAMARKAND
BACTRIA
KHOTAN
YU-T'IEN
KASHGAR
KUČA
TURFAN
TUNHUANG
WU-WEI
CH'ANG-AN

CHINA DURING THE HAN DYNASTY

North

▲ This map shows the route of the Silk Road that was opened during the Han dynasty when trade was first started. The traders' journey did not become safe until the Chinese armies had overcome hostile forts in the oasis towns of the deserts.

During the T'ang dynasty (AD 618–907), trade with the West increased because even more horses were needed for the army. By then China had perfected another product which became much in demand. This was porcelain and, in the ninth century, it started to be exported to India, the Middle East and Indonesia.

A group of foreigners make their way across China's long deserts towards the market towns of Ch'ang-an and Loyang where they will trade their products.

Transport

As the Chinese empire was so large, it was very important for the government in the centre to be able to communicate with the different districts in order to keep law and order. The First Emperor of the Ch'in dynasty (221–206 BC) realized this and forced millions of his subjects to build a vast network of roads and canals all over China. Low bridges were built over streams and rivers, and high ones between cliffs and canyons. In order to carry important government messages all over the empire, a system of courier stations was established where fresh horses were kept ready for relay. The Han and T'ang governments used the same efficient system for government communication.

Large barges were able to carry heavy loads along smooth, wide rivers, but smaller, lighter boats had to be used at difficult upstream parts of the Yellow and Yangtze rivers. Instead of returning downstream along the river, across dangerous rapids, these boats were often carried back over land to ensure their safety.

▼ Many different forms of transport were used in China during the Han and T'ang dynasties. Horses, oxen and donkeys would pull carriages and carry loads, as would camels. Rich families would travel in sedan chairs carried by two men. On the cover of this book, an emperor is being carried in a palanquin by four men. For the poor, the simplest and most useful vehicle was a wooden wheelbarrow. Men and women often carried loads from a long stick supported across their shoulders. How many different forms of transport can you see in the picture below?

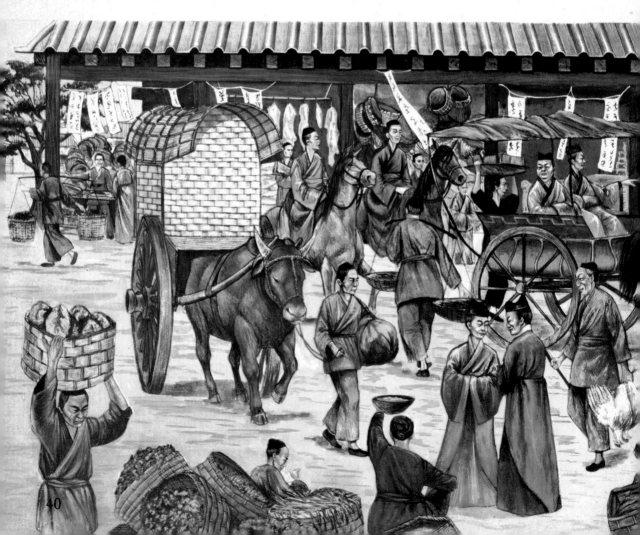

WATER TRANSPORT

◄ By the fourth century AD, large boats with stern-post rudders had been built to sail across dangerous seas.

► Some families lived in boats, rather than in houses. This 'house boat' has thatched roofing over the living quarters.

Buddhism

The Buddha, which means the 'Enlightened One', is the title given to an Indian prince called Siddhartha. Siddhartha was born in a small kingdom in India in about 560 BC. His father brought him up in great comfort and luxury but did not allow him to see much that went on outside their own house. Siddhartha therefore had not experienced other people's sorrows and suffering. However, one day he went out and noticed some peasants ploughing. He was moved to tears by the hardships endured by both the peasants and the oxen, and even by the killing of worms and insects by the plough. He decided to leave home and to endure pain and hunger himself while trying to think how the suffering felt by other people could finally be brought to an end.

Eventually he decided that extremes of pain *and* pleasure were both equally wrong. Salvation could be achieved if individual people followed a 'middle path' by not being selfish, ambitious, and wanting possessions. He began to teach these ideas to other Indian people. After he died, many of his disciples continued his teaching. A new religion, called 'Buddhism', had begun. Today Buddhism is one of the most widely spread religions throughout the world.

The Buddhist pilgrim, Hsuan-tsang (below), on his journey back from India. As he left, the king of India gave him a white elephant to carry the many Buddhist texts he was taking home. The Chinese emperor welcomed Hsuan-tsang back and built a special pagoda in Ch'ang-an (above) for the texts. Can you see this pagoda in the diagram on page 12?

▲ In the middle of the sixth century AD, images of the Buddha were cut out of some sandstone caves in Yun-kang. In Chinese sculpture, the Buddha either stands or sits on a throne. When he is standing (as on the right), he has one hand raised with the palm turned outwards, symbolizing that he is 'free from fear'. When he is seated, his hands may be joined together to show that he is thinking.

When China and India began to trade during the Han dynasty (206 BC–AD 220), Buddhism began to influence some Chinese people. However, the idea of leaving home to become a monk, and thus neglecting one's parents, was considered by Confucians to be a sin. Yet, by the T'ang dynasty (AD 618), the foreign religion had won a lot of followers. One of these was called Hsuan-tsang. After learning as much as he could in China about Buddhism, he decided that he had to travel to India to read some texts that were not available in China. Fifteen years later he returned to China with many Buddhist works which he translated into Chinese. This helped many Chinese people to understand the religion and to explain it to others.

Technology

The technology of ancient China was much more advanced than any other country's at that time. The amount China had achieved in technology by the end of the T'ang dynasty (AD 907) is a unique historical story.

In this book you have already learnt about the roads, canals and bridges that were built all over China; the city walls and fortifications, palaces and temples; the boats, carriages and efficient harnesses; the irrigation (watering) of land; the invention of gunpowder, spinning wheels and paper. Once paper was available, the Chinese gradually invented printing. To begin with, bronze and stone seals were engraved with important people's names. After ink was applied to a seal, the name could be stamped onto paper. (You have seen some seal marks on the painting of Lao-tzu on page 23.) Gradually woodblock printing developed, as shown in the pictures below. As a result, texts and books could be printed easily, rather than copied by hand, and more people were able to learn from them.

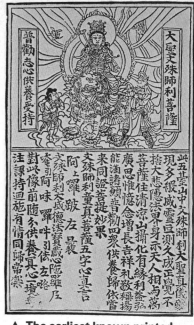

▲ The earliest known printed book, the Diamond Sutra, was produced in AD 868. The Buddhist text above was printed in the tenth century.

WOODBLOCK PRINTING

▼ 1 Chinese characters or drawings were brushed onto a piece of paper. A block of wood was covered with rice paste. While the ink was still wet, the paper was placed upside down on top of the block to stain it.

▼ 2 After the paper was removed, the wood around the stains would be cut away with an engraving knife.

▼ 3 A brush was then used to cover the raised surface of the characters with ink from an ink slab.

▼ 4 With a dry brush, the printer gently smoothed a piece of paper onto the inked characters to transfer them to the paper.

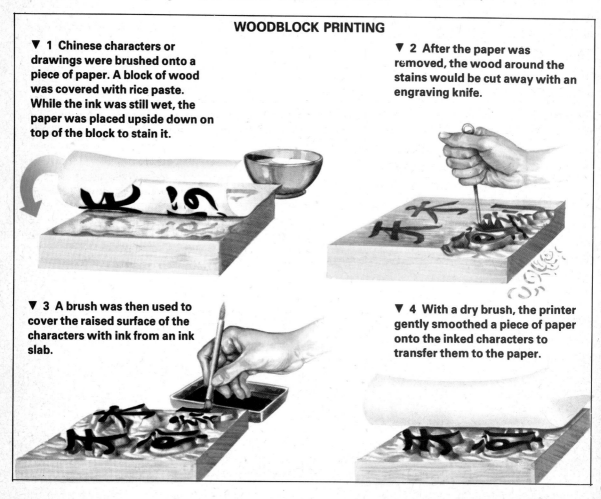

You have also learned in this book about the remarkable techniques the Chinese had for casting bronze into splendid vessels, tools, weapons and money. Iron was discovered in China in about 700 BC and skills were soon developed for smelting and casting it. As a result, the production of iron farming tools, and weapons, which were much stronger than bronze ones, increased China's food production and strengthened the army. Iron stirrups and wheels improved transport. The skilful Chinese methods of iron casting were not developed in Europe until much later.

Salt is a very important part of every person's diet. In the parts of China that were far from the sea, it was difficult to obtain salt. However, by the second century BC, a method had been developed for extracting salt from underground with the aid of steel drills. It could then be distributed to the main inland areas.

▲ Stone rubbings, like this one, were made in the tombs of Chinese people who were buried during the Han and T'ang dynasties. In the one above, salt is being lifted from underground with a long bamboo tube. A bamboo pipeline carries the salt to some iron pans for evaporation on top of the furnace on the right.

▼ In this early iron factory, the two men on the left are working bellows which blow air along an underground tube. From the tube, the air fans the flames below a furnace to the right. On the anvil in the centre, men are hammering solid iron into shapes.

Science and medicine

As Nature was so important to the Chinese, men who specialized in studying aspects of it, like the weather, the sky and magic, would play an important part in the government. The views of the Taoists were also highly regarded. By the end of the Han dynasty (AD 220), these different specialists had acquired much knowledge. With the help of men who knew a lot about technology, many clever scientific instruments were invented.

On page 18 there is a picture of a specialist choosing the site for a city with the aid of a magnetic compass. This compass originated during the Han dynasty (206 BC–AD 220). By the T'ang dynasty (AD 618–907), it had been developed into a very useful instrument for providing various scientists and travellers with directions. It was particularly used in the selection of new building sites (see page 18). Both sundials and waterclocks were being used in China by the early date of 100 BC.

A government official called Chang Heng, who lived from AD 78–139 during the Han dynasty, spent much time studying mathematics, geography, and the sun, moon and stars. He designed several instruments to help him with his work. These included a seismograph to record the direction of earthquakes, and an armillary sphere to help in the observation of stars and planets.

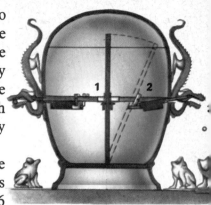

▲ The bronze seismograph which Chang Heng designed for recording the direction of the earthquakes that often occurred in China. During an earthquake, the pendulum in the centre (1) caused the arm (2) to open the mouth of the dragon on the appropriate side (3). This released a ball which would fall into the mouth of one of the frogs.

◄ An armillary sphere which was made out of a number of rings corresponding with the circular paths of stars and planets. It was used for measuring their movements in the sky.

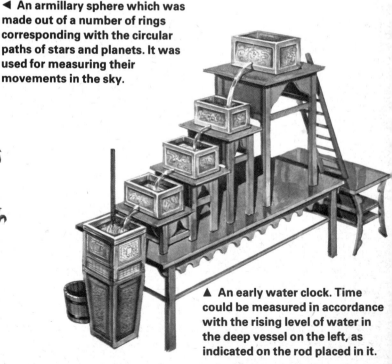

▲ An early water clock. Time could be measured in accordance with the rising level of water in the deep vessel on the left, as indicated on the rod placed in it.

◄ Herbs have been used in Chinese medicine from the very earliest times. On the left is Artemesia Moxa which is used in moxibustion. On the right is a type of mint which is used for relieving headaches.

▲ In moxibustion treatment, a special herb is burnt at points directly on the skin, or just above it, where the pain is felt. The painting shows a village doctor using moxibustion on a patient who is being held down.

► In acupuncture treatment, which has been used in China for more than 2,000 years, very thin needles are painlessly inserted into various parts of the body. This chart shows the correct pressure points to be used for both illnesses and operations.

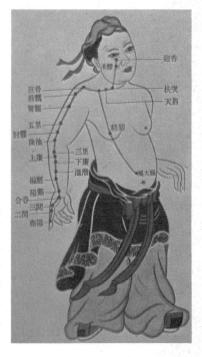

The early Chinese associated illness with an upset in the balance of Nature. During the Han dynasty, however, medical drugs and surgery were improved. Both acupuncture and moxibustion were applied to relieve pain and heal a wide range of illnesses. During the T'ang dynasty (AD 618–907), a book known as 'The T'ang Book on Drugs and Herbs' was written. The information in it was used as the basis of the most respected book on the subject today. From early times, the Chinese have realized how important it was to take exercise and therefore remain physically fit.

47

Death and the afterlife

When a person died in ancient China, his or her family, friends, and relatives gathered round to mourn. Children had to mourn for their parents for three years. They would wear white clothing to show their grief, rather than black.

It was believed that the dead people would live again in another world. They therefore had to be supplied with all the possessions they required for the afterlife. The kings of ancient China often ordered that their favourite courtiers should be killed and buried with them. But placed in the tomb of the First Emperor of China were thousands of life-size pottery soldiers, along with models of his palaces, and many precious goods.

The tombs of the rich nobles who died during the Han and T'ang dynasties contained numerous models of horses and chariots, and other useful objects, as well as servants, musicians, dancers, and so on. However, the common people could not afford such extravagant burials, if even a coffin. Instead, paper models of various possessions, including money, would be burned and offered to the dead people. The name of each person would then be added to the family's ancestor tablets, and his or her spirit would be worshipped along with the rest. Rich people sometimes bought whole hillsides for their family tombs. The farmers could bury their dead on their own land. Often a grave would be dug up after a few years. The bones were cleaned and then placed in a jar along a hillside.

▲ Tombs built during the Han and T'ang dynasties were tunnelled deep into the ground and made from very strong brick or stone. A number of carved, stone gates would be closed to cut off entry from one part to another.

◄ This frightening figure, made from porcelain, is a tomb guardian. He, and others, would have been placed in a tomb to ward off both evil spirits and robbers. However, much stealing from tombs did occur. Even the First Emperor's tomb was robbed.

► The dead bodies of a famous prince and princess, who died during the Han dynasty, were fitted into suits made from numerous squares of jade that were linked by gold wires. It was believed that this would preserve their bodies. However, in 1968 archaeologists discovered that their bodies had turned to dust.

A NOBLEMAN'S TOMB

Plan of a tomb of a rich nobleman who was buried during the Han dynasty. The Outer Gate leads through a long passage to the first stone gate which opens into the Front Hall. Through a second stone gate, the dead person's Audience Hall is reached. A Store Room is at one end and a Kitchen, lined with pictures of kitchen activities, is at the other. The Coffin is placed in the room opposite to the Front Hall. Parallel to the Coffin Area is a private apartment where the dead person could entertain his ghostly friends. Directly opposite that is the room where large models of his horses and carriages would be placed, with pictures of grand processions lining the walls. During this period pictures of other human activities, and of animals and birds, were often painted or carved onto the walls and ceilings of tombs.

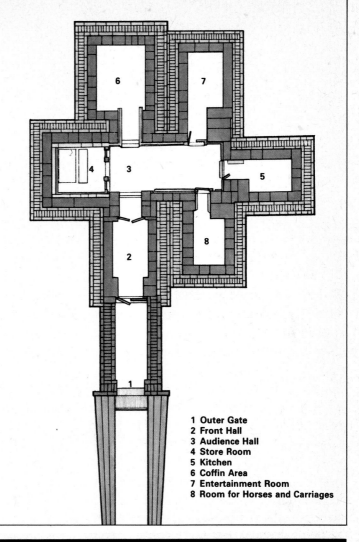

1 Outer Gate
2 Front Hall
3 Audience Hall
4 Store Room
5 Kitchen
6 Coffin Area
7 Entertainment Room
8 Room for Horses and Carriages

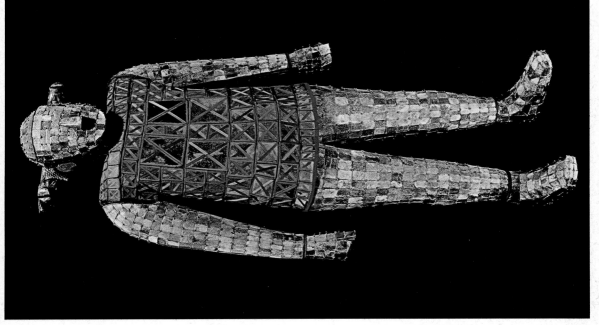

The story of ancient China (1)

?–about 1500 BC

There are many legends about the earliest Chinese. Some indicate that, by about 2850 BC, wise rulers were already teaching the people how to control the flooding of rivers, how to farm and trade and make silk and medicines. But there are no written records from these times and archaeologists have not found evidence yet to show that the rulers existed.

At first the people who settled in the North China Plain, along the fertile Yellow River valley, lived in small villages that were independent from one another. Gradually they discovered how to make bronze and, from bronze, weapons. When fighting broke out between villages, the people with the strongest weapons won. As time passed, one village leader won the most territory and became king over all the other villages. When the kingship was passed from father to son, the royal family's rule became known as a 'dynasty'.

It is said that the first king to establish a dynasty was called the King of Hsia. The first dynasty of China was therefore the Hsia dynasty. However, one of the king's descendants was very cruel to the people. At last they took up arms against him. Their leader became king and began the Shang dynasty.

about 1500–1027 BC

Because the first Chinese writing we know about dates from this period, we can say that Chinese written history began in about 1500 BC. Chinese archaeologists have recently discovered more evidence of the Hsia dynasty, but they have not yet found any written records. However, on animal bones and tortoise shells, they have found writing that dates from the Shang dynasty.

▲ The legendary king of the Hsia dynasty.

Under the Shang kings, the Chinese people became very skilled in bronze casting. They could cast bronze weapons in moulds, as well as many beautiful vessels that they used in religious ceremonies (particularly ancestor worship). They also knew how to carve jade and weave silk.

The king ruled with the help of many lords. The lords would give the king some of the crops that were paid to them by the farmers who lived in their territories. Each lord would also send soldiers from his own army to serve the king.

The last Shang king was very cruel. Eventually he was overthrown by another leader who ruled an area to the west of the Shang kingdom. This leader then became king over the whole area and began the Chou dynasty.

1027–221 BC

The kings of Chou ruled with the help of nobles (lords) who were either relatives or successful generals or ministers. They were given areas of land to control as states. Gradually these nobles became so independent that they ruled over their own states as kings. The king of Chou found that he had lost control over them. They began to take territory from their weaker neighbours and fight with other nobles. From 481–221 BC there was constant warfare and so this period became known as the 'Warring States'. The common people had to fight in the armies and therefore neglected their fields. Thousands died from the terrible conditions they faced.

The situation had to be improved. Consequently, some of the more educated people spent a lot of time thinking of new ways of government. Some of these thinkers gained a large number of followers. Influenced by Lao-tzu, many people withdrew from normal society in order to live more in harmony with Nature. They were called Taoists. Over the centuries many more people became influenced by Lao-tzu's theories. The man whose teaching later had the greatest and most permanent influence was Confucius (551–479 BC). But, at the time, the nobles were not impressed by his theories and turned to a different method of government. Strict laws were made and the people were threatened with harsh punishments if they did not do what they were told. The people who believed in this discipline were called 'Legalists'.

Eventually the state of Ch'in conquered all the other states (except for Yueh which remained independent because it was so far south). The king of Ch'in decided to unite China as an empire. He called himself Shih Huang Ti — the First Emperor.

221–206 BC

The First Emperor of the Ch'in dynasty built his capital at Ch'ang-an, which means Everlasting Peace. He hoped that his dynasty would last for 10,000 generations! The people regarded him, like all the previous kings, as the Son of Heaven.

With the help of his chief minister, who was a Legalist, the emperor ruled China with a firm hand. His main aim was to build up the power of the central government over the whole of China. He sent out officials to govern all the districts of China. He built roads, bridges and waterways so that they could all be reached when necessary. He kept up a very strong army. He also joined up all the main fortifications in the north into the 'Great Wall' so that northern tribes could not invade China.

In order to unite China properly, he made laws that weights and measures and customs duties should be the same everywhere. He also arranged for a standard index to be drawn up so that everyone used a common written language. Chinese writing could therefore be understood by all educated Chinese people.

▼ The Great Wall of China was constructed during the Ch'in dynasty (221-206 BC).

The story of ancient China (2)

221–206 BC (cont.)

In order to prevent scholars from interfering with his reign, in 213 BC the First Emperor ordered that all books should be burnt except for those dealing with necessary subjects like agriculture.

But the Ch'in empire did not last for long. The First Emperor died in the east of China in 210 BC. His chief minister, who was with him at the time, wanted to change the emperor's will so that a different prince would gain the throne. He therefore decided to keep the emperor's death a secret until he had done this. However, on the long and hot journey back to the capital, the emperor's body began to rot in the royal carriage. The chief minister therefore had to arrange for a cart of stinking fish to follow immediately behind the carriage so that no one would be suspicious. Not long afterwards, in the reign of the second emperor, rebellions broke out in various parts of China where the people had not liked his rule. After four years of struggle and bloodshed, a man called Liu Pang won over all the other armies and founded the Han dynasty.

▼ During the Han dynasty, foreign traders began to come to China along the Silk Road.

206 BC–AD 220

The new Han emperor ruled China through a central government but replaced the harsh rules with simpler ones. Helped by able officials and generals, he gradually restored order in the empire. He also encouraged scholars to voice their opinions again. Many of them followed the teachings of Confucius which gradually became respected all over China.

One of the greatest Han emperors, Wu Ti, reigned for a long time (141–87 BC). He took a very active part in the government and travelled over as much of China as he could. He began to appoint his officials through examinations. A university, and many new schools, were set up.

He also ordered one of his soldiers, called Chang Ch'ien, to travel westwards, beyond Central Asia, in order to find out more about foreign tribes and to trade. China's silk started to be exchanged for swift horses from the West. Eventually the Silk Road was opened and caravans of traders travelled along it from Tyre and Antioch on the Mediterranean, to Ch'ang-an. China became famous as far west as the Roman Empire. Through the Silk Road, Buddhism first came to China from India.

The Chinese army became much stronger through using crossbows. At different periods, it managed to conquer the hostile forts along the Silk Road that made it an unsafe highway.

During the Han dynasty there were many important inventions, like that of paper. There were also many advances in the fields of technology and science. China's territory expanded even beyond its borders during the Ch'in dynasty. It had become united as never before. The Chinese became very proud of all these achievements. No future dynasty prospered so much.

▲ Although Confucius lived during the Chou dynasty, his teaching was largely ignored until the Han dynasty when it was accepted all over China. He was then considered the greatest teacher who had ever lived. Portraits like this one were kept in nearly every school until the twentieth century.

AD 220–618

After the last Han emperor was forced to give up the throne in AD 220, there was much fighting between the various people who wanted to claim the throne. This civil war split China into 'Three Kingdoms' under the kings of Wei, Shu and Wu. Gradually, outside northern tribes managed to conquer the whole of North China and the Yellow River valley. This was the period called the North and South Dynasties (AD 316–581). In the north, northern chieftains reigned as emperors in Chinese fashion while, in the south, short-lived Chinese dynasties established themselves along the Yangtze River. In 581, the Sui family reunited China for the first time for $2\frac{1}{2}$ centuries. However, a rebellion brought their dynasty to an end in 618.

AD 618–907

Peace and stability were not restored until the T'ang rulers came to power. The man who was responsible for this became Emperor T'ai-tsung. He considered himself a 'Universal Monarch'. Under his rule, trade between Central Asia and the Middle East increased considerably, enabling Chinese influence to spread in all directions. Buddhism and other foreign religions were welcomed into China. A Buddhist monk, called Hsuan-tsang, went to India from China to study Buddhist texts.

The next emperor, Kao-tsung, was rather lazy and allowed one of his wives, Wu Chao, to deal with government affairs. When he died in AD 683 she took over all power as ruler. In AD 690 Empress Wu changed the dynastic name from T'ang to Chou. However, by AD 705 she was 80 years old and was forced to give up the throne. A few years later, when her grandson became emperor, the T'ang dynasty was restored to its former glory. Her grandson's reign was so splendid that he became known as the 'Brilliant Emperor'.

The T'ang dynasty is often referred to as the Golden Age of China. Unity revived some of the prosperity that was seen in the Han dynasty. At the same time, under the Brilliant Emperor, Chinese poetry and art flourished as never before. Chinese porcelain was perfected and exported far and wide.

Time chart

PERIOD	DYNASTY AND IMPORTANT EVENTS
from 2000 BC	**HSIA** The first dynasty of China is founded. The potter's wheel is introduced. Pigs, oxen, goats, sheep and dogs are kept on farms. More evidence of this period is being traced.
from 1500 BC	**SHANG** The Shang rulers establish authority over the settlements in the Yellow River valley. Large palaces are built in Anyang, the greatest of the Shang capitals. Irrigation is carried out. A system of writing is used to communicate with the spirit world. Beautiful bronze vessels are cast, and jade and ivory are carved. Silk is made. Armies use bows and arrows and wheeled chariots. Water buffalo are kept on farms.
from 1027 BC	**CHOU** The state under the Lord of Chou conquers the Shang. Civil war between different states begins and continues for almost two centuries. Known as the Warring States period (481 221 BC). Cast iron hoes, ploughshares, swords and picks are used. 'Breast strap' harness for horses invented, increasing their haulage capacity. Lao-tzu begins Taoism. Confucius introduces his theories.
from 221 BC	**CH'IN** The state of Ch'in defeats the other states. China becomes an empire under Shih Huang Ti, the First Emperor of China. The Great Wall of China is built. Roads, bridges and waterways constructed all over China. The same sort of money, weights and measures, and writing has to be used by everyone. 'The Burning of the Books'. (The First Emperor orders that all books, except those dealing with subjects like agriculture and the history of Ch'in, are burnt to prevent educated people from criticising his rule. Many scholars are also killed.)

PERIOD	DYNASTY AND IMPORTANT EVENTS
from 206 BC	**HAN** The Han leader wins power over the Ch'in. Confucianism becomes the state religion. Chang Ch'ien is sent to explore Central Asia. As a result, trade begins and the Silk Road is opened. Buddhist priests come to China. Spinning machines are used. Foot stirrups are invented. Powerful crossbows, with bronze triggers, are used. Salt is mined with steel drills. Stern post rudders are used on boats. Sundials and waterclocks used. Paper is invented. Chang Heng designs an armillary sphere and invents the seismograph.
from AD 220	**THE THREE KINGDOMS** The Han dynasty collapses during a revolt. China is divided into three kingdoms held by the kings of Wei, Shu and Wu. Continuous warfare.
from AD 316	**NORTH AND SOUTH** The north of China and the Yellow River valley are overcome by outside northern tribes. Buddhism becomes a popular religion in China.
from AD 581	**SUI** The Sui ruler reunites North and South China.
from AD 618	**T'ANG** The T'ang dynasty comes to power. Magnetic compass invented. Hsuan-tsang fetches more Buddhist texts from India. A Chinese Buddhist princess marries the king of Tibet. Empress Wu Chao rules from AD 683-705. Poetry, literature, art and music flourish. Woodblock printing begins. Gunpowder is used in fireworks. Polo is introduced from Persia. Porcelain is exported throughout Asia and the West. The Diamond Sutra is printed.
to 907	The T'ang dynasty collapses in AD 907.

The land of China

China's borders varied during the Han and T'ang dynasties according to the strength of their armies and the influence of the government in those areas. The far western border of the Han dynasty is shown on page 39; that of the T'ang dynasty is shown opposite. Important centres for trade or industry are also shown below.

Great Wall

Anyang

Yellow River

Loyang

Huai River

Ch'ang-an
(Sian)

Yun-kang
Buddhist caves

Yangchow

Nanking

Soochow

Hangchow

Chiang-chow

Ch'eng-tu

Yangtze River

YUEH

West River

0   1,000 km

Borders at the height of the Han dynasty (206 BC–AD 220)

Borders at the height of the T'ang dynasty (AD 618–907)

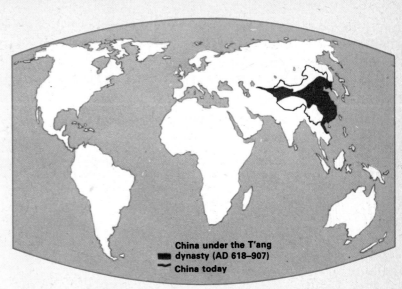

China under the T'ang
dynasty (AD 618–907)
China today

▲ This map shows the size of China during the T'ang dynasty, in relation to the rest of the world. It also shows how the area taken up by China today spread outwards from the T'ang area. With the extra territory, new groups of people became absorbed into the Chinese way of life.

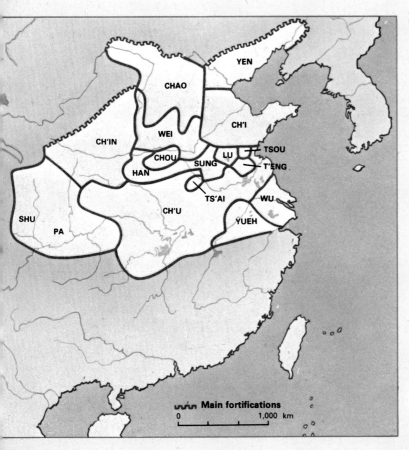

YEN

CHAO

CH'I

WEI

CH'IN

CHOU

LU

TSOU

HAN

SUNG

T'ENG

TS'AI

WU

SHU

PA

CH'U

YUEH

〰〰 Main fortifications

0   1,000 km

◄ During the Chou dynasty, a large number of states were created which were ruled by different families. They became very independent of the king and fought among themselves for extra territory and power. Eventually only seven states were strong enough to stand up to one another – Ch'i, Ch'u, Chao, Wei, Han, Yen and Ch'in. They became known as the Warring States. The states in the north built fortifications to protect themselves from outside invaders. When Ch'in finally won over the other states, and made China its empire, the main fortifications were joined together as the 'Great Wall'. The state of Yueh remained independent until the T'ang dynasty.

World history 1500 BC to AD 900

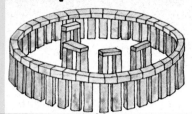

	China	Europe	Asia
1500 BC	The Shang dynasty rules China. A system of writing, in the form of picture symbols, is used. The techniques for bronze casting in China at that time have never been equalled. Beautiful bronze vessels still exist today. Irrigation is carried out. Wheeled chariots and bows and arrows are used.	The Minoan civilization in Crete is destroyed. The Mycenean civilization develops. The Greeks attack Troy. The Dorians invade Greece and destroy Mycenae. Central Italy is occupied by a tribe whose descendants are the Romans. Celtic invaders settle in Switzerland and France.	The Indo-Aryans arrive in India and set up an empire in the Ganges basin. The Aryan culture spreads to southern India, setting up the caste system.
1000 BC	The Chou dynasty has taken over from the Shang. Ironcasting begins so that better farming tools and weapons are used. The nobles become so independent of the king that civil war exists between them from 481–221 BC. Confucius and Lao-tzu introduce their theories.	The Etruscan civilization develops in northern Italy. Celtic invaders settle in France, Spain and Britain. The Druids are their priests, teachers and judges. Rome is founded in about 753 BC. The Greek states defeat the Persians in war. Alexander of Macedonia inherits the Greek Empire.	The Buddha is born in India in about 560 BC. Confucius is born in China in about 551 BC. In 516 BC, the Persians conquer the northern Punjab of India. Alexander the Great invades India unsuccessfully in 327 BC. Chandragupta Maurya becomes king. His grandson, Asoka, succeeds him in 273 BC.
200 BC	China is ruled as an empire by the Ch'in dynasty. The First Emperor orders that money, weights and measures, and writing are standardized all over China. The Great Wall is built. The Han dynasty takes over in 206 BC. Great advancements in technology, science and arts.	Roman armies conquer the neighbouring Mediterranean countries and invade Britain. Julius Caesar is assassinated in 44 BC. Augustus becomes emperor in 31 BC. Under Emperor Nero (AD 54–68) Rome is burnt down and many Christians are treated cruelly or killed.	In 185 BC, the last Mauryan ruler is murdered by his commander-in-chief who takes over the throne and starts the Sunga dynasty. Parthia annexes the kingdom of Taxila in 138 BC. In central India, much elaborately carved stonework is carried out.
AD 200	The Han dynasty collapses during a revolt. China is divided into Three Kingdoms. In AD 316 the north of China is conquered by outside northern tribes beginning the period of the North and South dynasties. In AD 581 the Sui dynasty reunites China. Buddhism becomes popular.	Emperor Constantine ends the persecution of the Christians. The Goths cross the River Danube and settle inside the Roman Empire. Gaul is invaded. The Visigoths, Suevis and Vandals set up their own kingdoms. Rome is sacked by the Vandals in AD 455.	The Kushans invade North India. Splendid Buddhist sculpture is carved in India. In about AD 405, the Japanese court of Yamato adopts the Chinese language. A Chinese Buddhist monk studies Buddhism in India. The king of Tibet marries a Chinese princess.
AD 700 **AD 900**	The T'ang dynasty expands China's territory and rules until AD 907. Chinese poetry and art flourish more than ever before so that the period is often referred to as the 'Golden Age'. More Buddhist scriptures are collected from India by a Chinese monk. Porcelain making is perfected.	Charlemagne's Holy Roman Empire is broken up. Invasion of Spain by Moslems in AD 711. In AD 732, they are overcome in France at the Battle of Poitiers. The Vikings sail across the North Sea and the Baltic. The first recorded expedition arrives in England in AD 787.	A short war breaks out between Tibet and China. Japanese leaders adopt Chinese culture. Buddhism also flourishes in Japan. The Japanese capital is established in AD 795 at present day Kyoto. It soon became one of the largest cities in the world.

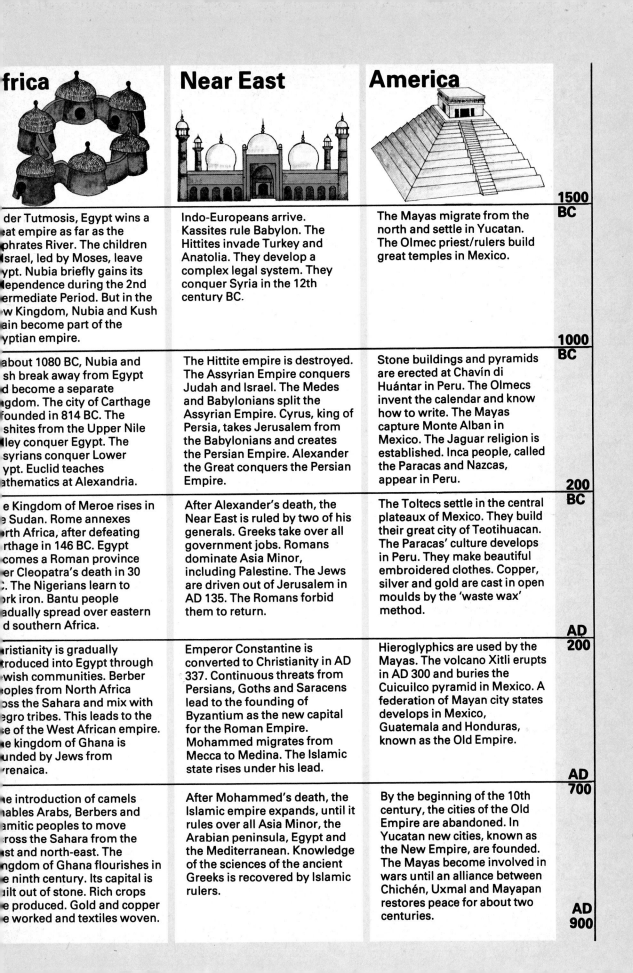

frica

Near East

America

1500 BC

Africa: der Tutmosis, Egypt wins a eat empire as far as the phrates River. The children Israel, led by Moses, leave ypt. Nubia briefly gains its dependence during the 2nd ermediate Period. But in the w Kingdom, Nubia and Kush ain become part of the yptian empire.

Near East: Indo-Europeans arrive. Kassites rule Babylon. The Hittites invade Turkey and Anatolia. They develop a complex legal system. They conquer Syria in the 12th century BC.

America: The Mayas migrate from the north and settle in Yucatan. The Olmec priest/rulers build great temples in Mexico.

1000 BC

Africa: about 1080 BC, Nubia and sh break away from Egypt d become a separate gdom. The city of Carthage founded in 814 BC. The shites from the Upper Nile ley conquer Egypt. The syrians conquer Lower ypt. Euclid teaches athematics at Alexandria.

Near East: The Hittite empire is destroyed. The Assyrian Empire conquers Judah and Israel. The Medes and Babylonians split the Assyrian Empire. Cyrus, king of Persia, takes Jerusalem from the Babylonians and creates the Persian Empire. Alexander the Great conquers the Persian Empire.

America: Stone buildings and pyramids are erected at Chavín di Huántar in Peru. The Olmecs invent the calendar and know how to write. The Mayas capture Monte Alban in Mexico. The Jaguar religion is established. Inca people, called the Paracas and Nazcas, appear in Peru.

200 BC

Africa: e Kingdom of Meroe rises in e Sudan. Rome annexes rth Africa, after defeating rthage in 146 BC. Egypt comes a Roman province er Cleopatra's death in 30 . The Nigerians learn to ork iron. Bantu people adually spread over eastern d southern Africa.

Near East: After Alexander's death, the Near East is ruled by two of his generals. Greeks take over all government jobs. Romans dominate Asia Minor, including Palestine. The Jews are driven out of Jerusalem in AD 135. The Romans forbid them to return.

America: The Toltecs settle in the central plateaux of Mexico. They build their great city of Teotihuacan. The Paracas' culture develops in Peru. They make beautiful embroidered clothes. Copper, silver and gold are cast in open moulds by the 'waste wax' method.

AD 200

Africa: ristianity is gradually troduced into Egypt through wish communities. Berber oples from North Africa oss the Sahara and mix with egro tribes. This leads to the se of the West African empire. e kingdom of Ghana is unded by Jews from renaica.

Near East: Emperor Constantine is converted to Christianity in AD 337. Continuous threats from Persians, Goths and Saracens lead to the founding of Byzantium as the new capital for the Roman Empire. Mohammed migrates from Mecca to Medina. The Islamic state rises under his lead.

America: Hieroglyphics are used by the Mayas. The volcano Xitli erupts in AD 300 and buries the Cuicuilco pyramid in Mexico. A federation of Mayan city states develops in Mexico, Guatemala and Honduras, known as the Old Empire.

AD 700

Africa: e introduction of camels ables Arabs, Berbers and amitic peoples to move ross the Sahara from the st and north-east. The ngdom of Ghana flourishes in e ninth century. Its capital is ilt out of stone. Rich crops e produced. Gold and copper e worked and textiles woven.

Near East: After Mohammed's death, the Islamic empire expands, until it rules over all Asia Minor, the Arabian peninsula, Egypt and the Mediterranean. Knowledge of the sciences of the ancient Greeks is recovered by Islamic rulers.

America: By the beginning of the 10th century, the cities of the Old Empire are abandoned. In Yucatan new cities, known as the New Empire, are founded. The Mayas become involved in wars until an alliance between Chichén, Uxmal and Mayapan restores peace for about two centuries.

AD 900

Glossary

acupuncture a medical technique for removing pain by inserting needles into specific points of the body.

ancestor one from whom a person is directly descended — for example, a grandfather.

archaeologist someone who studies the past from remains found in the ground.

armillary sphere an instrument used for measuring the movements of stars and planets.

banquet a feast which, in China, often consisted of as many as 12 different courses.

barter to trade, without using money, by exchanging one good for another.

customs duty a tax placed by the government on goods being sold between different states.

dynasty name given in China to a line of rulers from the same family.

to fallow to leave land unsown for a period after ploughing.

incense material burnt to give off a fragrant smell in the smoke.

irrigation watering of land.

kiln a large oven used for baking pottery.

moxibustion a medical technique for removing pain by burning a special herb directly on the affected part of the body.

paddy field a special field which can be kept flooded so that rice can be grown.

ploughshare the blade of a plough.

reconstruction an attempt to recreate something as it was in the past. A reconstruction can be a model, a painting, a building or an object.

seismograph an instrument for recording the direction of earthquakes.

shaman a special person who claimed to be able to communicate with spirits.

wards groups of houses that have been divided into enclosed areas.

Index

1 2 3 4 5 6 7—KP—86 85 84 83 82 81